Shut up and Listen

A Brief Guide to Clinical Communication Skills

Cathy Jackson

Dundee University Press

First published in Great Britain in 2006 by
Dundee University Press

University of Dundee
Dundee DD1 4HN

www.dundee.ac.uk/dup

ISBN 10: 1 84586 017 9
ISBN 13: 978 1 84586 017 2

Cartoons courtesy of Professor Geoff Gadd

British Library Cataloguing-in-Publication Data
A catalogue record for this book is available on request from the
British Library

Typeset by Creative Link
Printed and bound by Bell & Bain Ltd, Glasgow

Shut up and Listen

Contents

Half of the royalties from this book will go to

The Renal Unit
Yorkhill Children's Hospital
Glasgow

where I learned what a difference a person with good
communication skills can make!

Introduction

There's none so deaf as those who will not hear.

Anon

The title of this book, *Shut up and Listen*, refers to the two most important skills in clinical communication:

1. The ability to shut up or keep quiet and allow the patient to speak without interruption.
2. The ability to listen and truly hear what the patient is trying to tell you.

Even if you remember nothing else but these two skills from this book, you will have the basis of a good consultation.

This book has been designed as a revision aid to clinical consultation skills. It does not provide an exhaustive review of the literature on the subject, but if you know and practise the contents, you will not only have solid foundations for any type of clinical consultation but you should also be able to pass any undergraduate or postgraduate exam focusing on communication skills.

The book is suitable for *all* clinicians, including doctors, medical students, nurses, paramedics, dentists, pharmacists, midwives, health visitors, optometrists, occupational therapists, physiotherapists, radiographers (and probably a few more I haven't thought of!)

How to Use this Book

The bullet point lists at the beginning of every chapter will provide the 'skeleton' or bare bones of knowledge for that chapter. These should only be used for last-minute reminders, or for testing your knowledge.

The rest of the chapter will put a little 'flesh' on the bones and should let you make some sense of the whole subject. Suggestions for further reading are made at the end of the book for those who wish to discover the subject in more detail.

The first few chapters look at the general skills that are necessary for every type of consultation, while the last few chapters look at skills that might be needed in specific cases, such as giving large amounts of information.

It's no good having knowledge if you can't communicate it in a way that is useful to the patient, and it's no good having wonderful communication skills if you have no knowledge to communicate. You need both!

Most important of all, don't just wait for the exams – practise the skills as you read about them. They work in everyday situations as well as in clinical consultations, and the more you practise them, the more natural their use will seem. Bad communicators are those who have yet to learn and practise the skills!

CHAPTER 1

Before the Consultation

Before a consultation, consider:

- **The Right Setting**
  - Is this an appropriate place?
  - Is the room set up correctly?
  - Am I likely to be disturbed?

- **The Right People**
  - Am I the right person for this encounter?
  - Will I need another person with me?
  - Is this the right patient?
  - Will the patient need another person there?
  - Is there anyone here who shouldn't be?

- **The Right Knowledge**
  - Have I met this patient before?
  - Do I know the history of this patient?
  - Have I got all the results?
  - Do I need to look anything up before I see the patient?

It has long been recognised that you can influence any sort of encounter between two or more people by giving some thought to setting the scene beforehand. It is quite possible to make people feel uncomfortable or put them at their ease by small measures such as the careful choice and placing of various items of furniture. For any type of clinical consultation to be successful, patients have to feel comfortable with their surroundings, their physical position and the other people present. If you are aware of the difference that small changes to any of these things can make, you can set the scene for an effective and productive meeting for both you and your patient.

The Right Setting

Before any meeting with a patient, think about the setting and whether it is suitable for the sort of consultation that is about to take place. Will the meeting take place in a consulting room, at the patient's home, in a ward, or in an open or public place?

Consider whether your meeting needs to be held in a more public or more private place. In a busy ward at visiting time, nothing is more likely to attract attention from everyone present than the words: 'I understand you've been having problems with impotence, Mr Jones.' If necessary, change the setting – for example, on a ward, remember that bed curtains offer privacy only from peering eyes, not listening ears! It might be better if you can take the patient to a side room.

Is this a suitable place for this type of meeting?

Wherever the meeting is to take place, make sure that location is set up in the best possible way. Remove barriers such as tables and desks that are between you and the patient. If chairs are being used, make sure that all of the chairs are at the same height so that neither you nor the patient has a height advantage. If the patient *has* to be at a certain height, try and meet them at eye level: if the patient is in a bed, then sit on a chair next to the bed.

Wherever possible, try to make sure that you will not be disturbed, particularly when discussing sensitive issues or breaking bad news.

 Will the patient feel comfortable discussing medical problems in this setting?

The Right People

It is important to have the 'right' people at any consultation, if possible. This includes such simple measures as checking that you are talking to the correct patient – you would be amazed how many people don't do this, and what kind of problems occur as a result! Give some thought beforehand as to who should be present and why. Try and anticipate what will happen during the meeting and whether that should influence who should be there. Patients are unlikely to disclose their darkest secrets or innermost fears in the presence of ten students.

Before the meeting starts, consider:
- Are you the right person for this meeting?
- Do you need to bring anyone else with you, such as a chaperone or an interpreter?

- Will the patient be bringing anyone else along?
- *Should* the patient be bringing anyone else along?
- Will anyone need to stay with the patient after the meeting? (Think about situations in which you are going to give bad news.)
- Are there people present who ought not to be? (For example, a patient's visitors if on a ward; children, in cases where a procedure is to take place or sensitive issues are to be discussed.)

 Who should/should not be present?

The Right Knowledge

For any clinical relationship to work, a patient must have some faith in you and in your ability to help them. As a clinician, you must make sure that you have put yourself in the best possible position to do just that, and this includes gathering all the relevant information you think you might need *before* you start the meeting.

Consider:
- Have you met this patient before? Patients are unlikely to be impressed if they have met you before and you can't remember them or anything about the previous meeting.
- Have you got the right patient? Check!
- Have you read the patient's notes?
- Have you got the results of any investigations?
- Have you got the knowledge you need for this consultation?

 Do I have all the information I need for this meeting?

Once you have considered all of these things and have set the scene, you are ready for the patient.

CHAPTER 2

First Impressions

- **Setting**
  - What information does the setting give about you/the patient?

- **First Impressions**
  - ▸ **The Clinician**
  - What message is your appearance giving to the patient?
  - What is your body language saying?
  - How have you greeted the patient?

  - ▸ **The Patient**
  - What information can be gained from the patient's appearance?
  - What is the patient's body language saying?
  - How does the patient respond to your greeting?

In the first few seconds of any new encounter, early opinions are formed both by the patient and the clinician, and it is these early impressions which often set the tone for the rest of the encounter. If as a clinician you are aware of some of the elements which build this first impression, it is possible to adapt the setting, your appearance and your body language in order to send out the signals that you would *like* the patient to receive. The first few seconds of any clinical encounter can also give you very valuable insight into a patient's condition if you are observant and know what you are looking for.

Setting

The Clinician's Room

If the setting is a consulting room, have a look round with an objective eye to see the sort of things that patients might notice on first entering the room. An untidy room with evidence of previous patients in the form of blood and urine samples on your desk or unchanged linen on your examination couch may send out the message that you are not totally prepared to give the patient your undivided attention, or that your thought processes may be similarly disorganised. On the other hand, an overly tidy, sterile setting may mean that patients will not feel sufficiently comfortable to relax and be able to tell their full story.

There is no right or wrong way to arrange or decorate a consulting room, but be aware of the possible effects of any setting on people entering a room for the first time. The colour, light level and temperature of any room will be read almost unconsciously by those entering and will influence the way in which they respond. Interior design or lack of it will also give different impressions of the way in which you operate. Seating arrangements and the size and arrangement of other items of furniture may also influence how patients behave. For example, large, expensive desks with patients' seats some distance away from them would suggest that the clinician wishes to intimidate the patients and have them believe that he or she is important, powerful and in control, while an open seating arrangement with no desk between clinician and patient would tend to suggest that both parties are equal in standing. Again, there is no right or wrong – it depends on the situation and the message that you wish to convey. It is important, however, to be aware of the signals that you are sending out and to ensure that they are the right ones for the message you *wish* to convey.

Is my consulting room sending out the right messages about me?

The Patient's Home

If the clinical encounter takes place in the patient's territory – the patient's home, or bed space in a hospital – there is a wealth of information to be gained in the first few seconds by an observant clinician.

Is the patient's home warm and clean, or cold and neglected? Is the patient surrounded by other people's chaos and noise, or are they alone and silent? Are there any pets?

If the consultation takes place by the patient's hospital bed there may still be much information to be gained. Are there sweets or sugary drinks on the bedside table of a patient with uncontrolled diabetes? Has the patient shaved/put on make-up? Are there magazines or books around?

There may be many clues to a patient's state of health and wellbeing, and these may well appear to be at odds with what the patient actually says. For example, a patient who has brushed her hair, applied make-up and perfume and is sitting up in bed reading magazines and eating chocolate when you approach, yet tells you that she feels 'absolutely awful' when asked, may well have another agenda for staying in hospital – or a different definition of 'awful' from the one that most of us might share! Patients are frequently aware of the effects that appearance can have and may put an effort into changing it for an anticipated encounter, brushing hair or applying make-up for a ward round in the hope that they will look well enough to be sent home.

If a patient's appearance does not 'fit' with what you had anticipated, then ask others who see them more frequently if this situation is normal or unusual before drawing any firm conclusions.

Does what you see agree with what you hear from the patient?

First Impressions

Just as patients almost unconsciously take in the surroundings of the consultation room, they also make a quick assessment of 'you' in the first few seconds of your meeting, and the impression that they form of you in those first few seconds will, to a large extent, influence the rest of that encounter.

Clothes

There are probably as many ways of dressing and behaving amongst clinicians as there are clinicians, and, once again, there is no right or wrong way, as the requirements will change considerably with the setting. It is important, though, to realise what effects your dress and behaviour might have on your patients.

'I think I know precisely what to do here!'

The way you dress sends out strong messages about how you would like others to see you. 'Power dressing' was a phrase coined to recognise this, as well as the fact that clothes can be used to bolster our own and other people's ideas of our preferred status in any situation, for example by the use of formal and/or expensive clothes. The use of a more informal style of clothing conveys the message that, at the time we are wearing them, we prefer to operate in a more relaxed style. Most of us use different styles of dress in different settings, but it is worth considering, when choosing what to wear for the day, what type of encounters you are likely to have throughout the day and to dress in such a way as to influence others in the way that you want.

Body Language

Just as you are reading the patient's body language in the first few seconds, the patient will also be reading yours and deciding, on the basis of these few seconds, whether or not you are a good clinician, whether or not they can trust you and whether or not they like you. Greeting the patient by name, using good eye contact and a smile and making sure that the patient is comfortable before you begin to tackle the reason for the encounter is much more likely to give the patient a favourable impression of you than if you are still working at a computer screen – or, worse still, talking to someone else on the phone or on a ward round when you first come into contact with your patient.

 Are my clothes and body language giving out the right message?

Although first impressions will change over time as both you and the patient get to know each other better, it is important to know that they are formed in the first few seconds of any encounter and will determine how useful that first encounter is, for both of you.

CHAPTER 3

Gathering Information

- **Preparation**
  - What do I already know about this patient?
  - What might this patient want to talk to me about?
  - Have I met this patient before?

- **Setting**
  - Is the setting the right place for the encounter?
  - Is the consulting room set up in the best way?
  - Am I ready?

- **Introductions**
  - Am I able to give this patient my undivided attention?
  - What 'first impression' do I want to give this patient?

- **Gathering the Information**
  - Introductions if required.
  - Opening question or gesture.
  - *Shut up and listen!*
  - Silence.
  - *Shut up and listen!*
  - Reflect the patient's words back to them.
  - Summarise what the patient has told you.
  - Allow the patient to correct or add to your summary.

> - Ask the patient for their ideas, concerns and
>   expectations (ICE)
> - Set the agenda for the rest of the consultation.
> - Elicit more information using open then closed
>   questions.
>
> **Remember – *Shut up and listen!***
> - Oh, and don't forget to *Shut up and listen*!

Gathering information is one of the most important functions of any clinical encounter, wherever it might take place. The information gained may take many forms – establishing what the problem is, finding out how the patient is feeling on this occasion, or finding out what the patient knows, thinks or believes about their condition.

The key to gathering useful information is to provide an environment in which the patient feels comfortable giving the information, and to be aware that the only person who has the information that you want is the patient.

Preparation

What Do I Already Know about This Patient?

As with most consultations, a little preparation goes a long way. Spend a few moments looking at any notes you may have on the patient and finding out when they last came and what they came for. Have you seen them before? Are there any important features of the previous history that you should be aware of?

This sort of information may help to give you some 'feel' for the patient – for example, whether they come frequently with apparently trivial illnesses or whether they haven't been seen by anyone for the last ten years. It will also help to save the embarrassment of introducing yourself to a patient you have actually met several times before – the patient will remember you even if you can't remember them, and mistakes such as these in the early part of the consultation will undermine their confidence in your abilities to help them.

Setting
Is the Setting Right?
Not every consultation takes place in a dedicated consultation room, but wherever you are, check that the surroundings are as welcoming as you can make them and private enough to allow the patient to speak comfortably. Check that the furniture is arranged so that the patient won't feel threatened or intimidated: for example, chairs should be at the same height, and there should be no barriers, such as desks, between you and the patient.

If the consultation is taking place in a more public setting, such as a ward, ensure that there is as much privacy as possible, for example by drawing bed curtains. Be aware, though, that you may not get the same amount or type of information as you might in a more private setting, and if this is likely to be of some importance – if a patient appears to be upset, for instance – then it is well worth the effort of finding a more suitable place in which both of you can speak more freely.

Am I Ready?
Make sure that you have finished dealing with the last patient and tidied away all evidence of their consultation, such as bloods and paperwork.

Mentally prepare yourself for the next encounter. Most clinicians will deal with a wide variety of patients and problems within a short time. It is important to take a moment between each consultation to set aside the most recent encounter, and any emotions or frustrations that went with it, and compose yourself for the next patient. This will not only help you get through the working day, but it will give the next patient the impression that you are ready to give them your undivided attention for the duration of their visit.

Introductions
Your brief look at any notes will have reminded you whether you have met this patient before, and it may help you to remember a

previous consultation. If you have no record of meeting the patient before, introduce yourself both by name and by your position in the team, for example: 'My name is John Smith, I'm one of the nurses here at the practice.' Then check the name of the patient sitting in front of you: 'And you are Jane Brown, is that right?'

Don't address patients by their first names until you have been invited to: many people, both young and old, will take great exception to this. If you are unsure of the marital status of a female patient, don't be afraid to ask rather than offend by getting it wrong: 'Is that Miss or Mrs Brown?' Refer to them by the title they give, even if it is Ms!

Gathering the Information

Once you are sure that the patient is comfortable, whether on a chair in a consulting room or in a bed on the wards, you are now ready to begin the consultation.

There are an infinite number of ways to open a consultation for gathering information, and it is likely that during your training you will have seen some that are more successful than others. The opening question 'what brought you here?' is as likely to yield an answer such as 'the bus' as any statement about the presenting problem. More successful opening questions may include 'How can I help you today?' or, if you have seen the patient several times previously and you are helping them with a continuing problem, try 'How's things?', 'How are you doing', or the more minimalist 'So . . . '.

There are times when even just a gesture or facial expression can be used to signal to the patient that you are ready to hear what they want to tell you. Through trial and error, and practice, you will soon find a way of opening consultations that suits your preferred style. Exchange ideas with colleagues, and don't be afraid to try a new form of words. It is often very surprising what a difference changing the opening phrase can make to the rest of the consultation.

Shut up and Listen!

Whatever opening phrase or gesture you use, the most important thing you can do next is to listen to the response in a way that encourages the patient to speak.

Look at the patient as they speak, make eye contact if they will and use appropriate facial expressions, gestures and sounds to show them that you are listening. Be very aware of your body language. Fiddling with pencils, doodling or looking at a computer screen will all discourage a patient from talking, whereas leaning towards the patient, mirroring their position or adopting an open posture suggests that you are interested in what they have to say.

'Trouble sleeping? No problem – take two of these each night. NEXT!'

Watch the patient's body language as they are speaking, as it is frequently much more revealing than the words they are saying. A patient who is looking down, avoiding eye contact and playing with her rings as she is talking is likely to have a very different agenda from one who fixes you with his gaze and leans back in the chair with his arms folded across his chest.

Listen!

Listen to what the patient has to say. Allow them to completely finish talking before you say anything. You may feel after only a short time that you have grasped the problem and have enough information to want to start asking more directed questions, but if you do this, you will stop the patient telling their story and will have lost a lot of very useful information. Allow the patient to finish speaking without interruption: very few patients will talk for longer than two minutes, and it is a very useful investment of time.

Silence

When the patient has finished talking, resist the temptation to speak. Allow a silence to occur, and do not give in to the almost overwhelming temptation to fill it. Silence is very uncomfortable in this situation, and if you can resist the temptation to break it, it is likely that the patient will feel forced to do so instead. The information gained in this way is frequently *the* most valuable piece of information that you will gain, as the patient will frequently fill the silence with something they had been considering may or may not be worth telling you, or information that they hadn't yet decided to trust you with, or concerns that they hadn't previously spoken about.

Silence is uncomfortable, and the sorts of issues that are on a patient's mind are likely to be used to fill the silence. Very often, it will help to move the consultation along very quickly towards the most important agenda for the patient

Listen Again!

As the information the patient shares with you during the otherwise uncomfortable silence is likely to be very important to them, once again allow them to speak without interruption, and show them that you are listening.

Reflect What the Patient Says Back to Them

There may still be more that the patient wishes to tell you, or is concerned about, or hasn't yet put into words. Encourage them to continue by repeating back to them a part of what they have said to you and allowing them to take up the thread again. For example, 'Your best friend found a lump too, and it turned out to be breast cancer . . .' might elicit a response such as: 'Yes, and she had chemotherapy and radiotherapy and had a terrible time and only lived for six months after she was diagnosed.' Encouraging patients to continue in this way sometimes allows them to expand on what is really worrying them and helps you to know which direction a consultation needs to take.

Summarise
When you think the patient has told you everything they are going to tell you without any questioning from yourself, summarise the information that they have given you so far. For example: 'Let me check that I've got everything. You were in the shower last night and think you found a lump in your breast. You're not sure what it is and you'd like me to check it out. It doesn't hurt or anything, but you're worried because your best friend died from cancer of the breast after a miserable few months. . . .' Summaries such as this not only show patients that you have been listening to what they have been saying, but may also remind them of further information that they would like to give you, such as: 'Yes, and my grandmother had breast cancer too, but she died thirty years ago.'

Ideas, Concerns and Expectations (ICE)
Even though you may think it's obvious what ideas the patient may have about a problem and what concerns they should be having, you won't know that you're right unless you ask. Experience shows that you may be totally surprised by the answer.

Asking a patient for their 'ideas, concerns and expectations' is likely to result in blank looks, but over time you will develop your own style for uncovering this information. You can use questions such as 'Did you have any thoughts yourself as to what this might be?', or 'What is it that worries you most about . . . ?', or 'What are you hoping that I am going to be able to do for you today?' The information obtained from asking such questions may take you in a different direction to the one you had been planning, but is likely to help structure the consultation in a way that will most help the patient.

Set the Agenda for the Rest of the Consultation

Having heard the patient's story and discovered their ideas and concerns, you are now in a position to structure the rest of the consultation and, if necessary, plan for further visits.

If the patient has more than one problem or concern, acknowledge them all to show that you have been listening and are taking what they have told you seriously, and outline how you intend to deal with everything. For example: 'You've told me that you have found a breast lump and are very worried about that, and also that you need your blood pressure checking, and you think you might have a fungal infection on your foot. I think that's a little too much for us to tackle in one ten-minute appointment, so I suggest that we concentrate on the breast lump for today so that we have time to check it out thoroughly, and we'll make another appointment in the next few days so that we can check out the other two problems. Would that be okay?'

Outline the structure for the remainder of the consultation. This gives the patient some idea of what is going to happen and allows them to prepare themselves. Try something like this: 'I'd like to ask you a few more questions about the lump and your general health, and then examine you, if that's okay, and once I have done that, we can decide what we should do next.'

Elicit More Information

Fill in the gaps in the information you need by asking more questions. Start with general open questions such as 'Can you tell me a little more about . . . ' and close down to more specific questions as required.

Whenever possible, frame the question in such a way that the patient has to provide the answer. Ask 'How long . . . ?' rather than 'Does it last a few minutes?', or 'What does it feel like?' rather than 'Does it burn?' Information gained in this way is far more likely to be accurate than if the answer has been suggested to the patient. Closed questions may be used to get specific information if the patient has not volunteered it when given every opportunity. For example: 'Have you seen any blood?'

Interviews which have the sole purpose of gathering information should not exist. At the very least, the patient should receive an explanation of what is going to happen to the information they have given you, but more often the information-gathering phase forms only the first part of a consultation, which then moves on to giving information, making decisions, planning, etc., all of which are covered in later chapters. Information gathering is, however, a vital part of any consultation and it is worth mastering – if done well, it will help you to plan the remainder of any other type of consultation in the most efficient and effective manner possible.

Remember – *Shut up and Listen!*

The patient has the information you want, not you! If you are talking when you are trying to gather information, something is going wrong.

Oh yes, and . . .

CHAPTER 4

Giving Information

- **Preparation**
  - Do I have all the information I need?
  - Do I know enough to answer the anticipated questions?
  - Do I know where to get patient information leaflets?
  - Are there any relevant patient groups?

- **Setting**
  - Is this the right place to give this information?
  - Am I likely to be disturbed?

- **People**
  - Am I the right person to be giving this information?
  - Is this the right person to give this information to?
  - Should anyone else be present?

- **Giving the Information**
  - What does the patient already know?
  - What would the patient like to know?
  - Outline the areas to be covered (signpost).
  - Give the information in a logical sequence of small 'steps' or 'chunks'!
  - After each 'step' or 'chunk', check that the patient has understood.

- – Use everyday language rather than jargon.
- – Use pictures and diagrams.
- – Make the information relevant to your patient.
- – Summarise.
- – Ask patients if they have questions or would like further explanations.
- – Explore how patients feel about what they have been told.
- – Give leaflets/information sheets/web addresses, etc.
- – Repeat the 'take home message' just before the patient leaves.
- – Give the patient a route to return with further questions (the 'safety net').

Preparation

When you know in advance that you have to give results or other information to a patient, make sure that you have as much information as possible to hand. Check for outstanding results, try to anticipate what questions the patient is likely to ask in response to the information that you are about to give, and try to make sure that you have sufficient knowledge to be able to give answers. If you don't already have this knowledge, look up the relevant information or consult colleagues before seeing the patient.

If you are asked a question that you hadn't anticipated and don't know the answer to, don't be tempted to bluff your way out of it. Answer truthfully that you don't know the answer, but you will try to find out the answer before you see the patient again . . . and then remember to do it!

Know where you can access useful patient information leaflets about common and not-so-common conditions, either online, or in the practice or ward. Find out whether there are any useful patient groups that it might be helpful to tell the patient about.

Setting

Giving information effectively doesn't need to take a long time, but it does help if you are not disturbed while you are doing it. Avoid busy, noisy environments – such as the middle of a ward – and try to ensure you have as much privacy as possible no matter what type of information you are giving.

It is difficult for patients to retain large amounts of new information at the best of times, but receiving diagnostic information along with treatment plans and prognostic information from a doctor on a busy ward round who is surrounded by an entourage of nurses and students is far from ideal. It is likely to mean that the information will have to be repeated several times by many different people and may still be misunderstood or misinterpreted at the end of the process. It is much more efficient, and preferable from the patient's point of view, if you take a little longer and get the setting and the process right the first time round.

People

Information, particularly diagnostic information, should ideally be given by the person best qualified to give it, i.e. the person who already knows the patient. Although this may not always be possible, if you are giving any kind of information to a patient, you should always make sure that you have at least done the background reading and/or consulted with colleagues and know enough about the subject matter and the patient to make it a useful encounter for all concerned.

It sometimes helps, if the patient is willing, to have two people present when giving complicated information, as each person often remembers a different element of the consultation. Ask the patient if there is anyone they would like to bring along if you anticipate having to go over complicated information, and explain why, so that they are not alarmed.

Make sure, if the person you are giving information to is *not* the patient, that the patient has given you permission to share any information about them. Do not assume that because the husband/mother/son of the patient has asked for diagnostic/ treatment/prognostic information, they have an automatic right to this information. The patient's confidentiality must be respected at all times.

Giving the Information

What Does the Patient Already Know?

The first rule of giving information is to find out what the patient already knows. The main reasons for doing this are that it allows you to gauge how much information you need to give, where to start and how you can correct any wrong or misleading information the patient may have that could lead to misunderstandings.

If giving diagnostic, treatment or prognostic information, a simple question such as 'What have you been told already?' or ' Has anyone gone over the results of the tests with you?' will give you some idea what, if anything, has already been discussed, and will also allow you to fill in any gaps or correct any inaccuracies.

When explaining the course of a disease, further tests, etc, it is important to remember that the patient may already have obtained information from many sources, including other clinicians, family, friends or the internet. A simple question such as 'Have you heard of . . . before?' or 'What do you know about . . . already?' will help you gauge your patient's existing level of knowledge and understanding.

What Would the Patient Like to Know?

Not every patient wants to know every detail of every treatment and investigation. Some do, but some just want to know the 'bottom line'. The only way to know which is which is to ask. Asking 'Would you like me to go over your test results . . . ?' or 'Would you like me to explain a little more about . . . ?' will help you to find out how much your patient wants to know. However, important information – such as the risks involved, major side effects or different prognoses – that may alter a patient's management choices should be included in any explanation of the 'bottom line'.

Inform

How easily we remember information depends to a large extent on the way in which new information was given to us. For example, the eight-number sequence 81046122 would be challenging for most of us to remember for long without effort, but we would find it a lot easier to remember 2, 4, 6, 8, 10, 12, which uses the same eight numbers, but in a logical sequence.

The same can be said for any type of information: the more logical the sequence we are given, the more likely we are to remember it. It pays, therefore, to give some time and thought to the planning of the information you want to give and the best order in which to give it.

Having developed this plan, it helps the patient if you can share it with them, so that when they try to remember what you have told them, they recall the information under the general headings that you have provided. This is sometimes known as 'signposting' the consultation, and it could go something like this: 'I would like first to go over the results with you and explain what condition we think you have. Then I'll explain what options are available to you in terms of treatment, and once we have discussed those, we can decide on the next step.'

When discussing clinical information, it is easy to forget that, very often, we are quite literally not talking the same language as the patient and we may be using words that they do not understand. Medical students in their first year at university will frequently learn more new vocabulary than language students! Use language that is appropriate to the person you are speaking to – if in doubt, make it simpler rather than more difficult, as it is embarrassing and demeaning for a patient to keep having to say that they don't understand. Many will simply pretend that they have understood rather than ask you to explain what you mean.

Think of giving information as being similar to going downstairs with a toddler: if you run all the way down and assume that the toddler has followed you, the chances are that you will have to go all the way back up and start again, this

'Are you still with me?'

time coming down a step at a time and holding hands with the toddler. Similarly, if you give a patient all the information you have at one go and assume they have followed you, the chances are that you will have to start back at the beginning and take it a step at a time.

To save time for both you and the patient, take it a step at a time and give the information in small, bite-sized 'chunks', checking after each chunk that the patient has understood. This is sometimes referred to as 'chunk and check'.

Illustrate
A picture speaks a thousand words, and certainly diagrams can make information much easier to understand. Patients will often ask if they can take home the picture you have drawn for

them on the back of an envelope, as they can use it to help explain the information you have given them to members of the family.

Make Sure the Information is Relevant
Information is more easily remembered if it is relevant to the individual you are talking to and they are able to relate to it in terms of their previous experience. For example: 'The treatment we use for ulcers today means that, unlike your father, you won't need to have an operation and won't go on to develop the problems with eating that he had.'

When you have given all the information that you feel is necessary, and you have checked the patient's understanding, summarise the important points, bringing everything together. Even in the best circumstances, patients will only remember a small proportion of what they have been told, and summarising the important points in this way will help to make sure that it is the most important points they are most likely to remember.

How is the Patient Feeling Now?
Information can affect different people in different ways. Some will be happy that they have an explanation and a plan of action, while others will be worried about what is going to happen and how it will affect them. Always check how the information has gone down by asking, for example, 'How do you feel about what I have told you?' This will allow patients to raise any concerns or anxieties they may have, and may also help to demonstrate any misunderstandings.

Make sure that you give patients the time and space to ask any questions – some may need prompting, in which case you can ask them: 'Is there anything you'd like to ask me?'

'Take-Aways'
Give written information if you have covered a lot of ground during the consultation. This doesn't need to be pages of

information: bullet-point headings, diagrams or a few key phrases can all help the patient to remember what you have discussed.

Patient information leaflets can be useful, too, if you have them or know where to access them quickly online, as patients can read them at their leisure and clarify any points they were unsure of. Make sure, though, that you have some idea of their content before handing them over – make sure they are relevant and not likely to confuse patients.

Addresses for reliable websites can also be useful for some patients, as these sites often answer common questions that patients may not yet have thought of. If you give out good web addresses, it may stop patients from accessing less reliable or industry-sponsored sites that may provide biased information.

Take-Home Message

If the patient is likely only to remember a small amount of what you have said, it is important that you identify which bit of information is most important and go over it one last time just before they leave the room, signalling it with a phrase such as: 'Just to recap. . . .'

The 'Safety Net'

When any of us has been given a lot of unfamiliar information, it may take some time to digest it fully, and only later do we think of the questions we wish we had asked at the time.

Patients often only think of important questions once they have gone home or discussed with others what was said. It is important for them to have an opportunity to ask for more information or clarification of any points without feeling as though they are being a nuisance. A simple phrase such as 'You'll probably think of lots of questions you wish you'd asked as soon as you get home, and if you do, then just . . .' will reassure a patient that you understand this problem and are happy to help.

As an aide memoire for giving information, the 'lecturer's rules' can be very helpful:

- <u>Tell them what you're going to tell them:</u>
  'signpost' the general headings under which you intend to cover the information during the consultation.

- <u>Tell them:</u>
  give the information in plain language, small chunks at a time, and check the patient's understanding after each chunk.

- <u>Tell them what you've told them:</u>
  summarise what you've told them, and reinforce the key points.

CHAPTER 5

Helping Patients with Difficult Decisions

- **Preparation**
  - Do I have all the information I need about the options available?
  - Do I have all the information I need about the patient?
  - Have I developed a good enough rapport with this patient?

- **Setting**
  - Has sufficient time been allocated to cover all the options available?
  - Am I likely to be disturbed?

- **People**
  - Am I the best person to help this person make this decision?
  - Will the patient need help from anyone else to make this decision?
  - Would it help if anyone else is involved in this process?

- **Making the Decision**
  - What does the patient know already?
  - What would the patient like to know?
  - What role would the patient like to take in the decision process?

- Identify the options available.
- Explain each option in turn (see also Chapter 4, 'Giving Information')
- Avoid bias.
- Summarise.
- Does the patient have any questions?
- Allow time for the patient to think it over, where possible.
- Once the decision is made, why that decision?
- If you are happy that a 'fully informed' decision has been made, support the decision even if it is not the one you would have made.

Many areas of medicine are not black-and-white, and it is the 'grey' areas that can provide the patient with some very difficult decisions to make. If the choice is as simple as 'This medicine will cure you if you take it, but you will die if you don't', then the decision is a fairly easy one to make, but more often decisions are a process of weighing up the potential benefits of a treatment and the potential risks of the same treatment for any individual.

Difficult decisions not only apply when considering which treatment option to take – medicine versus surgery, for example – but may also apply to social circumstances, such as staying in one's own home versus moving into a care home. Helping patients to make informed decisions is very much an extension of the information-giving process, but the decisions that individuals make will depend on the way in which the information is presented to them. It is important for any clinician to be aware of this, and it is equally important that patients are helped to make the best decision they can, after being truly informed about all the options available in as unbiased a way as possible.

Preparation

To be in a position to be able to help the patient in any way, it is important that you have managed to establish a good rapport,

'Pain in the neck? If I were you, dear,
I would just cut it off!'

and that the patient feels able to trust you and your knowledge. It goes without saying, therefore, that you need to have the knowledge in the first place!

If you are unaware what options are available, or of the potential risks, benefits or implications of each option, then find out before you see the patient. Occasionally you may be caught unawares and will find yourself without the information that you feel you need. If you do feel that you need to find out more before discussing it further with the patient, don't be afraid to say so, for example, in the following way: 'Before we make any decisions, I'd like to do a little more research on the subject.' Patients generally respect honesty, and feel that you are taking an interest in them and their case.

Setting

Time set aside for a full discussion of all the options is time well invested. A hurried decision following a hurried explanation often results in a bad decision, and the repercussions of a bad decision may take much, much longer to put right. If well-planned and prepared for, even complicated discussions about difficult decisions can take place within a reasonable amount of time, and if the 'right' decision (for that patient) is made at the first consultation, this is a very effective use of time.

Try to make sure that you are not disturbed. It is very easy for both you and the patient to lose the thread of the discussion if there are interruptions. Also, provide an environment in which the patient can concentrate on your discussion. Minimise any distractions – for example, those that occur on a busy ward – or the presence of unnecessary people, such as on a ward round.

People

Consider whether or not you are the best person to help this patient make the decision. Someone with more experience may be better able to answer any questions from the patient, or, alternatively, they may feel more comfortable asking questions or voicing their concerns with someone from a different background such as a nurse, a physiotherapist, an occupational therapist, or a doctor.

When facing very difficult or potentially life-changing decisions, patients may wish to have present someone who they feel can act as their advocate. This may be a relative or friend, but it may also be another member of the health profession that they feel they trust to keep their best interests in mind when helping them to weigh up the pros and cons of all the available options.

Making the Decision

What Does the Patient Know Already?

Just as when you are giving information, it is important to find out what the patient might already know and might be thinking. If the patient is already well informed about all of the options available, it may be a waste of time, for both of you, to cover everything in detail again. The answer to a simple question such as 'Has anyone talked to you about this before?' might help you to gauge where to begin your discussion. If in doubt, or if you receive a vague response, the safest place to begin is at the beginning, with a summary of the situation as you understand it so far, checking after each step that the patient has understood.

What Role Would the Patient Like to Adopt?

Not every patient wants to know every detail about every treatment option. After finding out what your patient already knows, find out how much more they would like explained and whether or not they wish to be actively involved in the decision-making process. Some patients feel quite threatened or anxious at the prospect of making difficult or complex decisions and would prefer to be advised of the best course of action by someone they trust.

'Signpost' the Remainder of the Consultation

Once you have identified the areas that you are going to need to cover during your consultation, it will help both you and the patient if you outline a plan for the rest of the consultation. You can approach it something like this: 'Okay, I think what we need to do today is discuss your diagnosis in a little more detail and then have a look at the four options that you have for treatment before you decide what you might like to do next.'

Signposting in this way helps patients to know which areas are likely to be covered and allows them to prepare for the information that is coming, and also gives you a framework to work from, to make sure that all of he important areas are covered.

Identify the Options and Give the Information

Let the patient know about the choices that are available, and try to relate those choices to what you already know about the patient, but without making any assumptions. Don't assume, for instance, that just because the patient is a mother of young children she will want to get back to them as quickly as possible – she may prefer the option that allows her to spend longer in hospital, to give her a break!

Give the information in as clear a way as possible. Avoid using jargon, and if you feel it is helpful, use diagrams, models or other visual aids to help with your explanation.

Discussing options with patients can be very challenging. Clinicians often have many years of experience behind them, and during their careers might well have given some thought to what they would do if they were in a similar situation to their patient. It is always worth remembering, however, that the patient's priorities and concerns may be completely different from your own, and you should plan carefully in advance how you might avoid such bias when discussing the options available to your patient.

The manner in which any explanation is given will very much influence the message that is received by the patient. For example, if you say 'Fifty per cent of patients taking this treatment will get better', it is the same as saying 'Fifty per cent of patients taking this treatment won't get better'. The way in which it is framed will make a difference to the message that the patient understands.

It is important to remain as unbiased as possible when discussing choices. If, for example, you use factual statements concerning outcomes such as 'number needed to treat' (NNT – the number of patients who need to be treated with any particular drug in order for one patient to derive benefit) and can back up your statements with evidence where necessary, this will help to prevent problems at a later date if the chosen treatment does not work quite as well as might have been hoped.

After the Information
Your patient may well be reeling from all the information that you have given them, especially if there have been several options to consider.

Summarise all the important features, such as all the options and the pros and cons involved in each one. Ask the patient if there is anything further they would like to know about anything you have told them.

Find out how the patient is feeling and what their concerns are. Depending on the type of consultation, you may have covered areas that the patient hadn't been anticipating. This may have forced them to consider many possibilities that they hadn't even thought of before, which may give rise to a number of doubts or anxieties. It is important that the patient is given the opportunity to voice these in order to help them make the best decision for them.

The Decision

Allow the patient to come to the decision in their own time. Unless it is an emergency, offer them the opportunity to go away and think about it or discuss it with others. Give them a 'safety net' to allow them to come back with any further questions they may want answered while they are thinking over their decision.

When the patient has made a decision, it is worth asking why they arrived at that particular decision, particularly if it is not the one that you would have made under the same circumstances. The answer may tell you more about the patient and their particular circumstances that you didn't previously know, or may reveal that they have misunderstood what you have said. This will give you the opportunity to correct any such misunderstandings.

When you are happy that the patient has made a 'fully informed' decision, whatever that decision might be, it is important to support them in that decision to the best of your ability even if – or, rather, especially if – it is not the one that you would have made.This will help you maintain the working relationship and rapport for the future.

It is also important for patients to know that, wherever possible, if they decide that they have made the wrong decision and want to change their mind, they can come back and discuss this with you at any time in the future, as circumstances, priorities and anxieties may change with time.

- Do I have all of the information I need?
- Do I know what the options are?
- Do I know the pros and cons of each of the options?
- How can I frame the information in an unbiased way?
- Are there any information leaflets that might help the patient decide?

CHAPTER 6

Breaking Bad News

- **Preparation**
  Before the consultation make sure that you know:
  - Any results
  - As much as you can about the subject matter
  - What options are available
  - Who can help
  - What happens next.

- **Setting**
  - Ensure privacy.
  - Ensure adequate time.
  - No phones, bleeps, etc.
  - Think about room layout.
  - Have tissues ready!

- **People**
  - Someone senior who already knows the patient/carer/family.
  - Someone who can stay behind after you have broken the news.
  - Anyone the patient/carer would like with them.
  - No one else present – not during large ward rounds.

- **Breaking the News**
  - What do they know already?

- Warning shot.
- Break the news factually.
- Allow the news to settle – silence.
- Prepare for many different responses.
- What are their concerns/feelings/anxieties about the news?
- Check their understanding.
- Do they have any questions?
- Are they ready to consider options/make decisions/plan?
- Make sure there is a definite 'next step'.

• **Remember!**
- Your words will be replayed over and over again – try to get them right.
- There is *always* something that you can do to help.

Breaking bad news is a job that nobody likes doing, but it is important both for our patients and for ourselves that the process is made as painless as possible. When you give patients bad news, you are often changing their life completely and forever. Things will never be the same again for them, and they will remember and replay the conversation for a very long time to come.

The way that bad news is broken to a patient (or carer) will play a large part in the future relationship between yourself/your team and the patient and, in turn, the degree to which you are able to help the patient (or carer) in the future.

There is no magic way to give bad news, but giving thought to the consultation beforehand and having a framework for the meeting with your patient will make the experience less traumatic for both of you.

Preparation
Before giving bad news you need to ask yourself several questions. The first one is: 'Do I know everything I need to

know?' Familiarise yourself with the patient's notes and find out, for example, if they live alone, or if there is there any family history of similar problems. How long ago was the initial presentation?

What investigations have been done already? Make sure that you know all you need to know about your patient's condition, treatment options, prognosis and so on.

When you have considered all of these things, you are almost ready for the consultation. Before you meet the patient, though, take a moment or two to plan the structure of the interview, i.e., what you are going to say and how you are going to say it. Things don't always go according to plan, but even when they don't, it helps to have a framework to return to when necessary.

Setting

Bad news should be given in a quiet, private setting where patients can remain for a little while afterwards if they wish.

Bad news should, ideally, not be delivered in public on an open ward – and always remember that bed curtains only prevent others from seeing, not hearing.

Bad news should *never* be broken by phone, text, email or letter – and preferably not on a Friday afternoon, if there is no one available from the team for the patient to talk to over the weekend.

The interview is likely to take some time, so make sure that you have allowed sufficient time by, for example, making a double appointment (in a clinic setting), or ensuring 'protected time' (on a ward).

Make sure that there are enough chairs in the room for everyone present, and arrange them in such a way that there are no barriers, such as large desks or tables, between yourself and the patient.

There is nothing worse than being disturbed by a bleep or a phone when you have just told someone the worst news they are ever likely to hear. Give your bleep to a colleague, take the phone off the hook, and put a 'do not disturb' sign on the door.

'Now where was I before the phone
rang? Oh, yes – you've got cancer.'

People

Am I the Right Person to Give This News?

Whenever possible, the news should be given by a senior person
who has already developed a relationship with the patient,
preferably the person who initiated the investigations in the first
place and has sufficient knowledge about the subject matter to
be able to anticipate and answer any questions that may arise
during the consultation. At the very least, the news should be
broken by someone who already knows the patient and with
whom they feel comfortable.

Who Else Should be Present?

It is always helpful to consider, *before* you start the consultation,
who else should be in the room. You may wish to have someone
present who is able to stay with your patient after you have
delivered the bad news, such as a nurse, or a friend or relative of
the patient.

If someone has come to the consultation with the patient, or is sitting with the patient, don't assume that the patient wants them to join the consultation – it may just be a neighbour who has offered them a lift! Wait until the patient asks if their companion can come in too.

Large numbers of students, doctors, nurses or anyone else *should not* be present. This is a very private, sensitive consultation and *not* a public learning experience.

Breaking the News

Introductions

Unless you are both already well known to each other, begin by introducing yourself and anyone else that you have brought into the room. If there is a fellow health professional with you, explain their role, but be careful what language you use when doing this. 'This is Nurse X – she is our cancer specialist nurse' may cause considerably more alarm than: 'This is Nurse X – she is a specialist member of our team who is helping me today.' If there is anyone there who doesn't *need* to be there, such as a student, ask the patient if they would prefer that person to leave.

Make sure that you have got the right patient. It sounds obvious, but mistakes do happen! Also make sure that you know their relationship to anyone who has come into the room with them.

Starting Point

Find out first what the patient already knows. This will save you time if they have already been given the diagnosis by someone else, and it will allow you to have some insight into whether or not they may already be anticipating bad news. For example, the question 'I see you have had a number of investigations performed recently – has anyone discussed these with you yet?' could lead to a response 'No, that's what I'm here for today', or 'Dr X said there was a patch that didn't look quite right, and that he had taken a biopsy to see if it might be anything more serious, like cancer'. In either case, you know where you are going to have to start from.

Find out also how much the patient actually wants to know. Not all patients want to know everything in minute detail: some just want the 'bottom line'.

Warning Shot
Prepare the patient gently for what is coming by firing a 'warning shot', such as 'I'm afraid the news is not as good as we might have hoped'. This will alert your patient to the fact that there is something serious coming and will allow them to be slightly more ready for the news itself.

The News Itself
When you have arrived at this point, give the news in a sensitive, well thought-out, factual but easily understood way.

If the bad news is cancer, use the word 'cancer' – don't hide behind words such as growth or tumour, which may or may not be understood for what they are by the patient.

Give great thought to your choice of words. Don't forget: these words are going to be remembered for a long time by the patient, so make sure they are sensitive but unambiguous. Use short phrases, and don't give too much information initially. Once you have dropped the 'bombshell', the patient is unlikely to take anything else in at all for a short time.

Once you have delivered the news, allow the information to sink in – leave a silence or express empathy, but don't try to give any further information until the patient appears ready to receive it, which may mean waiting until another consultation.

Be prepared for any response. Patients may cry, remain silent, scream, become angry or show any other emotion. Always remember, however they react, that this is not directed at you but is in response to the news you have just given them. Try to be empathetic to their situation.

After the News

After you have given the news, allow patients to demonstrate their feelings. Ask them how they are feeling, or whether this has come as a shock. Listen to their response carefully, as it will often tell you a great deal about anxieties and concerns that you may not have anticipated. For instance, it may be that their major worry is 'Who will look after the cats?' when *your* immediate concern might have been 'What is the likelihood of successful treatment?' Never assume that you know what a patient is most worried about – experience will show that you rarely do!

Let the pace of the remainder of the consultation be dictated by the patient. Some patients will just want to leave the room and run home when they have been told bad news, while others may want to stay and discuss treatment options and management plans. Unless the patient is ready to listen, there is no point in continuing to discuss what the next step might be. Gauge whether or not they are ready by asking a question such as: 'I have just given you some bad news, which may well be enough for you to deal with today. Would you like to go home now and come back tomorrow, or would you prefer me to continue for a little and talk about the possible choices you have for the next step?'

If they choose to go to the next step, give them a 'map' of the rest of the consultation by saying something like: 'We need first to talk about the things we need to decide this week, and then we will have a look at the options for treatment in the longer term and the advantages and disadvantages of each. Lastly we need to arrange for you to be seen by Mr Y, and I will answer any questions you may have.' This kind of 'signposting' helps the patient to remember information, as they can follow the logical sequence of events.

Give information in small amounts. (See Chapter 4, 'Giving Information'.) Check that your patient has understood what you have said, and ask if there are any questions that they would like to ask you.

Many people find it difficult to tell their partners or children the news accurately, so it is often helpful to offer to tell family members, or to be available to answer any of the family's questions, if that is what the patient would like. Offer contact numbers that patients can ring if they think of any questions or queries when they get home.

Always, always, always find something positive for patients to hold onto, even if the news is as bad as it can possibly be. No situation exists where we can do nothing at all for a patient. Make your patient aware that whatever lies ahead they are not alone, and that you and the team are there to support them and face the challenges of the disease with them.

After the Consultation

After the consultation, make an accurate note in the patient's records of the areas discussed. This will allow others involved in the patient's care to be aware of the stage that the patient has reached in the process.

Breaking bad news is never easy and can be very traumatic for those breaking the news as well as the patients. Be aware of the effect that delivering bad news can have on you as a professional, and after any consultation of this nature, take a few minutes to reflect on how it went, which parts appear to have gone well, and how you might improve on the parts that did not go quite so well. Gather your thoughts before continuing your work with other patients.

Lasltly, discuss with colleagues consultations in which bad news has had to be broken, and learn from each other's experiences.

CHAPTER 7

Discussing Sensitive Issues

- **Preparation**
  - What do I already know about this patient?
  - Do I have all the information I need?
  - Do I know enough to answer the anticipated questions?
  - Do I know where to get patient information leaflets?
  - Are there any relevant patient groups?

- **Setting**
  - Is this the right setting for this consultation?
  - Will the patient feel sufficiently relaxed in this environment to discuss this issue?
  - Am I likely to be disturbed?
  - Do I need a more/less private setting?

- **People**
  - Am I the right person to be discussing this topic?
  - Do I need a chaperone or witness?
  - Is there anyone present who perhaps should not be?

- **Discussion**
  - ▶ **Gathering Information**
  - Allow patients to give their account without interruption.

- Use an open question or reflection of what has been said to invite more information.
- Give warning of any sensitive questions, and add that they may not be relevant.
- Summarise, and allow the patient to fill gaps.

▸ **Giving Information**
- Signpost the areas likely to be covered in the consultation.
- Give the information professionally and factually, but with sensitivity.
- Assess the patient's 'starting point' knowledge of their condition.
- Correct any misconceptions.
- Use non-judgemental language, and avoid making statements personal.
- Be prepared for a range of responses, and understand why they may occur.
- Empathise and reinforce helpful behaviour.
- Use humour if appropriate.
- Work in partnership with the patient to agree a plan of action.
- Summarise, provide written information and allow for further questions.
- Put a 'safety net' in place.

Preparation

As with any consultation, a little preparation goes a long way. Plan how you might approach the discussion, as a little forethought could save a lot of problems later. Have a look at the patient's notes beforehand, and try to get some feel for how the patient might respond to what you have to discuss with them. For example, a seventy-year-old spinster's reaction to being told that she has a sexually transmitted disease is likely to be very different to that of a sexually promiscuous homosexual male.

Make sure that your knowledge base is adequate to cover any

questions that you might reasonably anticipate, and know where you can access further information, should you require it. Patient leaflets and the details of patient support organisations are always useful to have to hand in this situation, as in any other type of consultation.

Setting

When you know that sensitive matters are likely to be discussed, it is important to ensure that the setting is suitable. No patient is going to want to enter a full and frank discussion of anything remotely sensitive during a business ward round with curious neighbours on either side, or on an open ward at visiting time with bored visitors hanging on your every word. It is *your* responsibility, if you are initiating the discussion, to make sure that there is sufficient privacy for the patient to feel comfortable enough to take a full part in this discussion. If you are delivering sensitive information, then you have a duty of confidentiality towards the patient to make sure that you do so in privacy.

People

In everyday life, we are all aware that there are some people we trust enough to confide in, and others with whom we would be very reluctant to share even very basic factual information. Patients are no different. Patients must feel they can trust the person they are speaking to and that whatever information they put forward will be received by the health professional in a non-judgemental way. For this type of consultation, it is particularly important that a good rapport has developed between clinician and patient so that the patient feels comfortable taking part in the consultation, as well as to prevent any misunderstandings that might result in potential conflict.

If you don't believe that you have developed this kind of rapport with your patient, you may wish to consider whether there may be a more appropriate person to initiate the discussion. If there is no such person available, you may wish to consider bringing along another member of the team to the consultation, in case the patient misinterprets what you say and is offended or insulted by it.

If the patient has brought a companion to your meeting, consider whether or not their presence might inhibit the discussion at some stage. For example, it is possible that a teenager might feel unable to give a truthful account of recreational drug use if a parent is present, or a woman may not want to discuss the imminent break-up of her marriage if her children are playing at her feet. It is sometimes not enough to ask if the patient if they are happy for the person to remain in the room, as they may not be aware of the direction in which you are planning to take the discussion. If you think you might need to ask for potentially sensitive information and it would not be appropriate for anyone else to be with the patient when that happens, consider ways in which it might be possible to arrange to see the patient alone – by moving your patient into a separate room to conduct an examination, for example, or by arranging to see them alone at a later date.

Discussion

Gathering Information on Sensitive Issues

The skills needed for gathering information are the same as those needed for any other type of consultation (see Chapter 3, 'Gathering Information'), but there are one or two additional points to think about when discussing anything of a sensitive nature.

During the discussion, the patient will constantly be deciding whether or not they are prepared to share information with you, and they may well tell you something they have never told anyone else before. It is vital that you don't interrupt their story, as, once interrupted, they may not carry on where they left off, and you may lose important information forever.

The use of silence will often encourage the patient to tell you even more. Silence between you and patient is extremely uncomfortable, and if you can resist the urge to fill the silence it forces the patient to fill it instead. The sort of information that patients will use to fill a silence with are pieces of information that they had been thinking about but hadn't yet decided whether they were ready to share with you. If silence forces them to speak, it can be one of the most revealing moments of the whole consultation and often provides invaluable information.

In a nutshell, then – *Shut up and listen!*

Once you have heard all that the patient wishes to tell you, summarise and reflect their words back to them to encourage them to continue with their story, as you would in any other consultation.

If, after hearing all that the patient has to tell you, there are still gaps in the information you require, gradually move from open to closed questioning, as in other types of consultation. If you reach specific, sensitive areas that you need to enquire directly about, it is worth remembering that some questions may in themselves cause offence to some people. Sexual history and recreational drug use are obvious examples, but many people may be offended if they are even asked whether they smoke or drink. Many questions that make up a normal social history can cause problems in certain communities, and it is worth taking this into consideration when taking any type of history, even just a routine clerking history.

To avoid causing offence, it is often helpful to fire a 'warning shot' that you are moving into a sensitive area, explaining that you are about to ask general questions that form part of a routine history and asking permission to move into that area of questioning. You could say something like this: 'There are a few questions that I need to ask everybody with this condition, and they may not apply to you, but I should ask them anyway. Would that be okay?' This allows the patient to prepare for what might be coming, and also explains that you are not making a judgement about them or their likely behaviour but instead following a routine line of questioning.

Giving Information on Sensitive Issues

We've all been there – we have all at some time thought: 'How on earth am I going to tell them. . . .' I am referring to the sort of problems that are not in themselves bad news – at least, not what we as professionals might think of as bad news – but are the sort of diagnoses that might cause embarrassment or offence to the patient, which in turn means the diagnoses are likely to cause us some anxiety too. In medicine, there are all sorts of 'problem' diagnoses, such as sexually transmitted diseases, poor personal hygiene, unusual social habits and head lice, with many others in between. Patients are all different, and what will cause great embarrassment to one may be considered trivial by another.

The initial part of the consultation, as with any other, will help you decide how best to proceed, as it will give you a chance to gain some idea of the type of person you are dealing with. A harassed mother of five is likely to respond very differently to a high-flying businessman to the news that she has head lice, but appearances can still be deceptive.

Start by asking the patient for their ideas about what the problem might be. If they have already arrived at the correct conclusion, it makes the remainder of the consultation considerably easier for you. For example, the businessman might surprise you by saying: 'I think it might be head lice – I was visiting my grandchildren last week, and they have all picked it up from their school.' If, however, the patient tells you they have no idea what they might be suffering from, or has arrived at a completely wrong conclusion, this too will help you to gauge how to proceed.

Once you have discovered the patient's starting point, signpost the rest of the consultation, as you would in any other, in something like the following way: 'Okay, what I'd like to do is explain what I think the problem might be, why it might have occurred and what we can do to help.' Have a plan or framework in your mind for how you are going to give the information – and remember that embarrassment is infectious. If you are embarrassed, the patient is likely to become embarrassed and anxious too. Be sensitive to the feelings of the patient, but deliver the diagnosis in as factual a way as possible. Give the information without blame and without making it personal. For example, rather than saying 'Your cut has become infected because you're filthy and you could do with taking a bath once in a while', try 'Cuts sometimes become infected when bits of dirt get in them, and it often helps to try to keep the area clean by bathing at least once a day until the area is completely healed.' The message might be almost the same, but the second statement is much less likely to cause offence.

Empathise with their situation wherever possible, and reinforce any helpful behaviour. For example: 'Yes, it must be tough after a hard day working in the fields, and I can understand why you might just want to fall into bed, but you did the right thing coming to see me about it. Now we can treat it before it turns into something more serious.'

Humour can be useful to lighten the atmosphere if the patient is looking anxious, but use the knowledge you gained about the patient during the initial part of the consultation to judge how it might be received.

People may react in different ways when receiving sensitive information, and it helps to be prepared for a range of responses. Reading the body language of the patient as you are giving the information will help you to gauge their likely response. Some may become defensive or angry, but always remember that these responses result from feeling guilty, embarrassed or uncomfortable. Respond by being empathetic, allowing them to voice their concerns and correct any misconceptions

After giving any sensitive or embarrassing information to a patient, work with them to arrive at and agree a plan of action, both in terms of their treatment and any behavioural changes that might be desirable. Summarise the consultation, provide written information where appropriate, and allow the patient to ask questions.

Consultations which involve sensitive issues can cause embarrassment and anxiety all round, but actively listening to patients, developing their trust and providing an environment in which they can feel comfortable discussing any problem all lay the foundations for a successful and productive consultation. Being non-judgemental and making statements that apply generally rather than being personal also help to make the patient (and therefore yourself) feel more comfortable during the discussion. Avoiding censure and embarrassment allows you develop a working relationship and continuing rapport with patients, which allows you to help them in the most effective manner – which, at the end of the day, is what is most important!

Shut up and listen!

- Is this topic likely to cause offence?
- How can I phrase the information in a non-personal and non-judgemental way?

CHAPTER 8

Helping Patients to Give Up (Smoking, Drinking, Eating, Drugs)

- **Preparation**
  - What do I already know about this patient?
  - Has this patient tried to 'give up' before?
  - Do I know what services are available which might help this patient?
  - Have I developed a good enough rapport with this patient?

- **Setting**
  - Is this an appropriate setting for this discussion?
  - Has enough time been allowed to do justice to this subject?

- **People**
  - Am I the best person to help this patient?
  - Is there anyone the patient would like/not like to be present?

- **Helping the Patient Make the Change**
  - If you are doing all the talking, you are lecturing – stop it!
  - Shut up and listen!
  - Hear what the patient is saying.
  - Identify the state of readiness to change:
    - ▸▸ Pre-contemplation

▸▸ Contemplation
▸▸ Planning
▸▸ Action
▸▸ Maintenance (or relapse)
- Pitch your discussion at the correct level of readiness to change.
- Move the patient forward to the next state using 'motivational interviewing'
  ▸▸ Express empathy
  ▸▸ Develop discrepancy
  ▸▸ Support 'self-efficacy'
  ▸▸ Roll with resistance
  ▸▸ (Avoid conflict)
- Be non-judgemental
- Praise any step made in the right direction, however small.
- Don't give up on patients if they don't succeed at the first attempt

Preparation

If you are hoping to try to help a patient change any type of behaviour, it is helpful to know as much as you can about that person before you start. If you have known the patient for some time, you may already have some idea as to what makes them tick, but even if you are meeting them for the first time, it is helpful to read through the notes first to get some feel for the nature and extent of the problem before you see the patient.

The sort of information it is helpful to look for is:

- Any health problems that the patient may have developed as a result of their current behaviour.
- Whether or not they have tried to change before and if so, what happened.
- Whether there is more than one form of behaviour that it

would be desirable to change – and, if so, some idea of which one it might be best to tackle first.

- Whether there is any family history that you should be aware of, e.g. asthma, ischaemic heart disease, cerebrovascular disease, cancer, etc.
- Occupational and other social history.

Setting

Most often the first stages of helping a person to change will take place during a consultation about some other problem, and effective progress can be made in a relatively short period of time. Wherever possible, though, it is helpful to set aside sufficient time to discuss the problem, so that as a health professional you do not feel constrained by a full waiting room outside. If time pressures do not allow for sufficient discussion on the first occasion, offer the patient the opportunity to return if they feel ready to tackle the problem.

People

Health behaviour can be a very sensitive topic to many people, and it is important to realise that however much you want to help your patient, you may not always be the best person to do it. To discuss the problem openly and gain some faith in your ability to help them, the patient must trust you and your ability to understand the problem. It is very important in this, as in all other types of consultation, to establish a good rapport with the patient.

Consider whether or not there are people in the room who should not be there, or whether the presence of other people might actually be helpful. For example, it is not helpful to have a spouse in the corner of the room saying 'I've been telling him for years he should give up, but will he listen? I might as well be talking to a brick wall', but it might on occasion be helpful to have a nurse, pharmacist, doctor or other health professional present who has a special interest in this area.

Helping the Patient Make the Change

'Do you smoke?' As soon as we ask this question we can almost hear the patients thinking: 'Here we go again!' All too often patients have had lectures about their smoking or drinking and they are almost prepared for the inevitable to happen again. The fact that it *does* happen time and time again shows that lecturing patients on their vices, as a tactic for health behaviour change, doesn't work.

'If you don't give up, you'll die, you know!'

Whether or not a patient 'gives up' will depend on whether or not they see the need to, whether they want to, whether they feel able to and whether they are ready to try.

In order to help them, we need to know the answers to these questions first, so, rather than starting off with a statement such as 'You need to give up smoking, it's bad for your heart', an open question such as ' Have you ever tried to give up smoking?' will tell you whether or not they have ever seen the need and have tried to change, and might even give some insight into why they failed.

The 'States of Change' model[1] is a useful tool to use when deciding the level at which to pitch your discussion. This model describes several states of readiness to change, from never even having considered changing through to the maintenance of a successful change in behaviour. Finding out a person's state of readiness to change will at least help you to engage the patient at an appropriate level. For example, saying to a patient who has already tried to give up smoking several times, 'You should give up smoking it's not good for your health' is only likely to meet with irritation, but if you ask 'Have you ever tried to give up?', they can begin to tell you their story.

It is important to remember that when using this model, except in extreme circumstances, it is very unlikely you will ever be able to move a patient from 'never having seen the need for making a change' to 'successfully making a change' in the course of one consultation. Your aim for a single consultation should be to move them along one stage, for example from thinking that

States of Change Model[1]

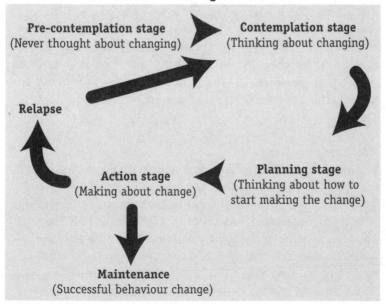

Pre-contemplation stage
(Never thought about changing)

Contemplation stage
(Thinking about changing)

Relapse

Action stage
(Making about change)

Planning stage
(Thinking about how to start making the change)

Maintenance
(Successful behaviour change)

they really ought to give up smoking to actually planning when and how they might go about it.

Once you have discovered where to pitch the discussion, the next question is how to actually move the patient along to the next stage.

Are You Lecturing?
Remember:

- The only person who can make the decision to change their behaviour is the patient.
- The only person who can make the change in their behaviour is the patient.
- The only person who knows why they haven't managed to do it before is the patient.
- The only person likely to make a realistic plan to make it work this time is the patient.

The message from these reminders is that if you are doing all the talking, you are lecturing, and it isn't going to work. Yet again, the most useful tactic to employ is to 'shut up and listen' as the patient tells their story, makes their excuses, tells you about all the people who have tried to make them stop/carry on smoking, or whatever. The more information you have about a patient, the more likely it is that you might be able to help them.

Motivating to Change
When we are deciding to do or not do something, whatever that something is we make a decision about the potential risks and benefits of each decision. The role of 'motivational interviewing' is to try and persuade the patient to acknowledge that the potential benefits of changing their behaviour outweigh any potential risks and therefore help them to begin the process of moving to the next stage.

A four-step process to help motivate individuals towards

changing their behaviour was described by Miller and Rollnick in 1991.[2] The four steps are described as:

Express Empathy
Allowing patients to tell their stories will help you to see what difficulties they have had and to gain some understanding of the problems they may be facing and how you may be able to offer help or support. For example, a statement such as 'It must have been really difficult to try and give up when all the rest of your family were still smoking' shows that you have a) been listening and b) are trying to understand. If you can show the patient that you are trying to see things with their eyes and trying to understand, it will help to strengthen the rapport between you and may make the patient more receptive to any gentle challenges you might make about their lifestyle or beliefs.

Develop Discrepancy
Listening to what a patient is telling you will help you to identify differences between how they would like their life to be and how it actually is. Make a mental note of any of these discrepancies as they occur and use them to help the patient find their reason to begin to make the change. For example, the statement 'I don't get out as much as I used to – now I'm unemployed I can't afford to anymore' might provide the sort of ammunition you need to help a smoker or drinker find the motivation they need to move to the next stage.

Support Self-efficacy
What this phrase actually means is to help the patient believe that they *can* do it.
Many patients will give up before they have even tried just because they believe that they can't do it, don't have the willpower, or whatever. Again, the more you know about a patient, the more you are in a position to help – you may be able to point out other areas in which they have managed to succeed, or you may be able to help them set small, achievable

targets which will support the belief that perhaps they can do it after all! For example, 'Give it your best shot for a week and then come back and tell me how you got on' might have a more positive effect than giving your patient a month's supply of a tobacco substitute and advising that if they need more, all they need to do is ring up for a repeat prescription.

When a patient has made a step in the right direction, however small, give the praise that the patient will feel is deserved. Finding out that a smoker has cut down from twenty a day to seventeen a day may not be earth-shattering, but it may well have taken that patient a great deal of effort and willpower. If you ignore this achievement, why should they bother to do more? But if you say, 'Well done, that's the first step, that's always the most difficult. I wonder how far you'll be able to go this week?', their achievement has been noted and rewarded, and the patient may just rise to the challenge of continuing.

Roll with Resistance
This phrase might be better reworded as 'explore the reasons for resistance'. If a patient is beginning to come up with reasons why change is not possible or not needed, it is often valuable to find out why they are putting up barriers to change. Rather than meet the patient head-on, it can be very revealing to ask 'why?' or 'why do you say that?' This will encourage your patient to talk about the barriers, and often, in so doing, they will realise just how ridiculous their arguments appear and may begin to develop their own solution to the problem.

Behavioural scientists sometimes talk of a fifth principal of motivational interviewing and that is avoid conflict. This is really an extension of exploring any resistance. If you feel that you have hit a brick wall in the discussion, rather than point out that the patient is totally wrong in holding a particular belief (even if they are!), it is more productive to ask why they hold that belief and get them talking again. Remember, only patients can make the decision to change their behaviour – simply telling them that they 'have to' is not going to work. Allowing them to tell you why they think they don't need to might be very revealing.

Conflict is always destructive to the clinician–patient relationship. Rapport deteriorates, and with it any chance you might have of being able to help patients help themselves – which, at the end of the day, is the whole aim of the exercise.

Shut up and listen!

- If you are doing all the talking, you are lecturing – stop it!

- States of change:
  - Precontemplation
  - Contemplation
  - Planning
  - Action
  - Maintainance (or relapse!)

- Four (five) principles of motivational interviewing:
  - Express empathy
  - Develop discrepancy
  - Support 'self-efficacy'
  - Roll with resistance
  - (Avoid conflict)

Notes

1. Prochaska, J.O., DiClemente, C.C., and Norcross, J.C. 'In search of how people change'. *Am. Psychol.* 1992; 47:1102–04.

2. Miller, W. and Rollnick, S. (1991). *Motivational Interviewing: Preparing People to Change Addictive Behavior*. New York: Guilford Press.

CHAPTER 9

Dealing with Aggressive and Violent Patients

- **Preparation**
  - What do I already know about this patient?
  - Has this patient been violent before?
  - Is there any history available from anyone else?

- **Setting**
  - Where is the exit?
  - Is there anything between you and the exit?
  - Is the room layout suitable?
  - Are there any potential weapons lying around?

- **People**
  - Should anyone else be present?
  - Is there anyone present who should not be?

- **Body Language**
  - Be aware of your own body language.
  - Be aware of the patient's body language.
  - Fear versus Anger.

- **Defusing the Situation**
  - Remain calm.
  - Speak in a calm measured tone.
  - Develop rapport.
  - Allow the patient to 'blow'.

- *Shut up and listen!*
- Sit (if it's safe to do so).
- Be non-judgemental.
- Acknowledge patient's feelings.
- Ask patient to tell their story.
- Be very aware of your/their body language.

- **If It All Goes Very Wrong**
  - Stay calm – if you panic, they will.
  - Be very, very aware of your /their body language.
  - Never turn your back.
  - Know how to summon help.
  - Know where your escape route is.

- **If It All Goes Very, Very Wrong**
  - *Run!*

Preparation

It is not always possible to anticipate when a patient is likely to be angry, but when there is some indication that this might be the case, forewarned is definitely forearmed.

Find out what you can about the patient before you see them, either from the notes or from relatives or neighbours if you have been called to an 'incident'. Things to consider are:

- Does the patient have a history of angry outbursts?
- Has the patient been violent in the past?
- Is the patient likely to be under the influence of alcohol or drugs?
- Is there any past history of mental illness or physical illness, such as a brain tumour or diabetes, that may account for the patient's behaviour?
- Is the patient likely to be very frustrated by recent events?

Setting

If the consultation is taking place in a consulting room, prepare the room in advance for both your benefit and the patient's. Arrange the furniture to provide a relaxed environment, with no barriers such as desks between you and the patient. *Always* make sure that it is *your* seat that is nearest the door. Check the room for any items that may be used as missiles or weapons in the wrong hands, such as scissors or heavy ornaments, and remove them from sight. Know how to summon help should you need it, and make sure you know where your exit is.

If you have been called to a patient's home or other setting, the same principles apply – i.e. try to make an informal seating arrangement, with your seat nearest to the door, and always, always know where your exit is.

People

Whether or not there should be other people present during the consultation will vary with the situation. This is one type of consultation where it can be much easier to control what is happening if there is only you and the patient in the room. If, for safety's sake, the police or other agencies need to be close at hand, it will help to defuse the situation if they are not visible to the patient – for example, standing to the side of an open door and outside the room. On occasion it *may* help to have another person present, if it is a member of the family or a friend that the patient feels able to trust and who is able to remain calm and appear relaxed in the face of anger and rising tension.

Body Language

Body language is important in every type of consultation, but at no time is this more the case than when consulting with angry and potentially violent patients. In this situation it is absolutely essential to be aware of your own body language and manipulate it to give out signals which will help to defuse rather than escalate a tense situation. The message that you need to send out is that you pose no threat to the patient – this will help them to relax a little and offer a smaller threat to you.

It is very, very important to do this consciously, because the signals you will give out as someone who is frightened are similar to those you might give out if you were about to go on the attack, and they are therefore liable to misinterpretation by a patient in a very high state of alertness. This would have possibly disastrous consequences.

Body language that may send out the wrong signals and escalate the problem:

- Defensive posture – arms folded across chest.
- Any attempts at height gain over the patient – e.g., rocking or standing very upright.
- Hands in pockets with thumbs out, or arms folded with thumbs up – appears cocky or aggressive.
- Hands locked into a fist – ready for attack.
- Fixing their gaze – confrontational.
- Large hand gestures – may be misinterpreted as an attack.

'. . . and another thing . . .'

Body language that may help defuse the situation:

- Put yourself at a height disadvantage – i.e. sit, if safe to do so.
- Stand or sit side-on to the patient rather than directly in front of them.
- Make eye contact, but don't fix their gaze; look down from time to time.

As well as your own body language, be aware of the patient's. Look for possible signs of impending attack, such as:

- Increased restlessness.
- Erratic movements.
- Increase in muscle tone.
- Pacing around the room.
- Appearing to see or hear a third party.

Defusing the Situation

It's not what you do but the way that you do it, and not what you say but the way that you say it!

How you react to the patient will make a huge difference to how they react to you. Keeping calm and giving the appearance of being relaxed will allow the patient to see that you pose no threat and will help them to relax a little too. Ask the patient if they would like to sit and, even if they decline, sit yourself if it feels safe for you to do so (tip – don't cross your legs, as it is more difficult to get up in a hurry if you need to). By giving the height advantage to the patient, you are reinforcing the message that you are not a threat.

If the patient is still angry, allow them to 'blow' and get rid of their anger. Don't interrupt their flow until they have finished completely, and then reflect back some of their words and try to encourage them to tell more of their story. You could say, for example: 'You said it was one big cock-up from start to finish – tell me a little more about what happened.'

Encouraging the patient to talk and showing that you are listening will help to develop a little trust and improve the rapport between you. Yet again, using the SHUT UP AND LISTEN technique will help you to survive the consultation!

When nervous or frightened, there is a tendency to speak quickly and at a higher pitch, so make a conscious effort to slow down your speech and bring down the pitch. As in any other consultation, try to identify the patient's concerns and anxieties, show empathy where you can and be non-judgemental at all times. Show your patient the same respect as you would any other, and offer your support to try and move the problem forwards.

If It All Goes Very Wrong

If the signals that you are reading from the patient are telling you that your strategy isn't working, and, if anything the situation is worsening – don't panic! Stay calm. If you panic, the patient will, and their actions may then become more unpredictable (or, in some cases, all too predictable). Be prepared to start from the beginning and allow them to 'blow' again. As fear and panic begin to rise in you, your body language will change and those changes will instantly be recognised by the patient. Make a conscious effort to control your body language and speech.

Try to engage the patient in conversation, acknowledge their concerns and ask for more information about their situation or problem.

Know how to summon help, and keep a clear path between you and your exit. *Never* turn your back on a potentially violent patient.

If It All Goes Very, Very Wrong

Run for it!

Any consultation such as this may leave you a little traumatised. Take a few minutes for yourself after it has all passed, and use the time to reflect on how it went and how it might have gone differently. Talk to colleagues and share your experience with them – they may be able to learn valuable lessons for the future. Always make detailed and accurate notes of the consultation immediately after it has happened – if the patient is threatening or irrational, these notes may prove invaluable for both you and others.

- **Where is the exit?**
- **It's not what you do but the way that you do it!**
- **It's not what you say but the way that you say it!**

CHAPTER 10

Consulting through Interpreters

- **Preparation**
  - What language/dialect does the patient speak?
  - What age/gender is the patient?
  - Does the interpreter understand medical terminology?
  - Allow at least two to three times as long as normal for the consultation.

- **Setting**
  - Arrange seats so that the interpreter is sitting at your side.
  - Ensure no interruptions.

- **People**
  - Is there anyone in the room who should not be?
  - Is there someone else who should be in the room?

- **Before the Consultation**
  - Introductions.
  - Ask for correct pronunciation of patient's name.
  - Any cultural differences in body language that you should be aware of?

- **The Consultation**
  - Introductions and explanation of roles.

- Outline the procedure.
- Use no jargon.
- Speak in short phrases.
- Address the patient directly.
- Read the patient's body language.
- Avoid superficial consultations.
- Questions, ideas, concerns, expectations.
- Respect the patient's privacy during any examination.
- Thank the interpreter and respect their professionalism.

The increasing movement of workforces across countries has meant that many of us consult with patients who do not have English as a first language. Although many of these patients can 'get by' in everyday life, understanding the nuances of medical information or making important, life-changing decisions with only a limited knowledge of what has been discussed is another matter entirely. It is our responsibility as health professionals to ensure that what we are saying has been fully understood by patients, and for that reason, amongst others, it is important that we use professional interpreters rather than friends or relatives of the patient.

Patients who may not have sufficient English for a medical consultation often bring their own 'interpreter' with them. Clinical consultations that use these unofficial 'interpreters' are not to be encouraged and are fraught with problems for the following reasons:

1. The person translating, although they say that they speak both languages, may not have sufficient experience or vocabulary to translate accurately. Rather than say 'I don't understand what you mean', they are more likely to translate what they think you might have said – which may be something entirely different! Unless you speak both languages, you wouldn't know if there were wild inaccuracies in the translated version.

2. Similarly, you cannot be sure that the patient's words are being accurately related to you. Friends, and especially relatives, may sometimes change what is being said to suit their own agenda.

3. The patient may not have realised the sort of questions that you were going to ask when they volunteered a member of the family or a neighbour as translator. For example, they may not have realised that a complaint of abdominal pain might lead to a menstrual or sexual history being taken, and the person who is doing the interpreting may be too embarrassed to translate either the questions or the answers, or both.

4. There is no guarantee of confidentiality for the patient when using a member of the same community as an interpreter, and this may restrict what the patient feels able to tell you.

5. There may be a lack of professionalism on the part of the unofficial interpreter, and there will certainly be no indemnity. As the health professional, it is your responsibility to ensure that an accurate history has been taken and that the patient has fully understood what you have said. It is therefore your responsibility to arrange for a professional interpreter to be present and you are the person likely to suffer the results of any litigation if a problem occurs as a result of the lack of a common language between yourself and your patient.

Preparation

When arranging for an interpreter to be present, it is important to make sure that the interpreter is a suitable one. Make sure that the interpreter actually speaks the same language as the patient, and the same dialect. (People in Surrey and Glasgow both apparently speak English, but that doesn't necessarily mean they will be able to understand each other!) Wherever possible, try to match the age and gender of the patient and interpreter to help the patient feel able to speak more freely.

Interpreters, like other professionals, specialise. When arranging for an interpreter, ask for one who is experienced in medical translation as they are more likely to be able to understand and translate any medical terminology.

Translation takes time. Each phrase used by both the clinician and the patient will need to be repeated at least once, and therefore the consultation will take at least twice and often three times as long as when using only one language. If no allowance is made for this at the time of booking the appointment, it will result either in an unsatisfactory consultation or a number of very annoyed patients sitting in the waiting room.

Setting

The seating arrangement is particularly important when consulting through a third party. When someone speaks, our natural tendency is to look at them. If both interpreter and patient are sitting in front of you, your head will move from side to side as if watching a game of tennis. If you seat the interpreter at your side, and out of your immediate view, it will allow you to concentrate your full attention on the patient, even when it is the interpreter that is speaking.

The natural rhythm of a consultation is lost when consulting through interpreters, and it requires a degree of concentration to keep the discussion within the usual framework. Any interruption will make this much more difficult, and it will help if distractions from other people, phones, bleeps, etc. can be minimised.

People

Although the consultation is taking place through an interpreter, in all other respects it should be treated in the same way as any other consultation. Thought should be given as to who should or should not be present in the room, using the same criteria as usual.

Before the Consultation

It is helpful to meet the interpreter a few minutes before the patient arrives. During this time, make use of their expert knowledge of cultural differences and ask if there are any common differences in everyday customs that you should be aware of, such as shaking hands or making eye contact. Check that you have the correct pronunciation of the patient's name and by which name it would be appropriate to call them (family names and given names do not always occur in the same order).

The Consultation

Introduce yourself and the interpreter. If the patient has brought along a friend or relative, explain tactfully why you will be using an interpreter.

Make sure that both the patient and the interpreter understand that they can interrupt at any time to ask for clarification of anything that they have not understood.

'Could you ask her, I mean him, if she, I mean you . . .'

Choose your language carefully, avoiding jargon, and speak in short phrases at any one time. Wait for the interpreter to complete translating a phrase before speaking again. This will allow the interpreter to interpret accurately, without forgetting what has been said.

Always address your questions directly to the patient, saying, for example, 'do you . . .?' rather than 'does she . . . ?' The patient should be the focus of the consultation at all times, even when the interpreter is speaking.

Be aware of the patient's body language, and remember that although the patient may not feel sufficiently confident to conduct the whole consultation in English, they may be able to understand a considerable amount of what you are saying.

The patient has the right to the same quality of care as any other patient. Consultations through a third party are more challenging that normal, but don't be tempted to take shortcuts by conducting a superficial consultation. Explore the patient's concerns and expectations as you would for anybody else; indeed, it is often more important to do so, as your line of questioning may reveal anxieties or expectations that you could not otherwise have been aware of, due to possible cultural differences with respect to healthcare.

If you need to examine the patient, respect the patient's privacy, but keep the interpreter close at hand to explain what you would like to do, making sure to obtain consent. A bed curtain to screen the patient is often sufficient for this purpose, or a door kept slightly ajar.

At the end of the consultation, summarise and ask the patient if they have any questions. Ask the interpreter to write down any important information for the patient to take away, and check that the patient can read it!

If a further appointment is required, arrange it there and then at a time suitable for all three of you. This will allow for some continuity and will help to develop a degree of rapport between the interpreter and the patient, making the process easier for both.

When the consultation has finished, discuss any cultural issues you may be unsure of with the interpreter, thank them for their help and show them the respect they deserve as fellow professionals.

- Have I made sure of the best seating arrangement?
- Is the patient always the focus of my attention?
- What would I do next if this was a 'normal' consultation?

CHAPTER 11

Exam Checklists

Preparation

Just as with consultations, a little preparation goes a long way when it comes to sitting exams. Having a basic framework in mind will help you keep on track both during a consultation and in an exam situation.

The main framework of a consultation will be very similar for most consultations, with only small differences depending on the nature of the discussion. When revising or preparing for an exam, learn the main headings of the framework and the rest will easily fall into place.

If all else fails, during an exam, remember that the patient is the most important person involved in the consultation – they have the story to tell and they are the ones that are affected by any information you might give them (in OSCE examinations, often the 'patient' also awards marks to each candidate depending on their opinion of how the consultation went from a patient's point of view). Remember the 'NICE' patient (**N**eeds, **I**deas, **C**oncerns, **E**xpectations), and this will help to keep your consultation patient-centred.

The following pages outline the features that are likely to be present on an examiner's checklist for the commonest forms of communication-skills testing found in OSCE examinations. Remember that OSCE exams represent an artificial situation and often involve 'simulated' rather than real patients. Many OSCE examiners will not have had any recent specialist training in communication skills and will be marking against a written checklist. For this reason, make sure that each stage of your OSCE consultation is extremely obvious: for example, it may not feel completely natural for you to ask a patient if they have any ideas or concerns about what their condition may be, or what they are expecting from the consultation, but it will earn the tick in the box and more marks on the marking sheet.

Basic 'History Taking'

- Greeting – greets the patient by name/checks they have the right patient.
- Introduction – introduces themselves and anyone else in the room and explains their roles.
- Presenting complaint.
- History of presenting complaint.
- Systematic enquiry.
- Social and lifestyle history.
- Family history.
- Drug history – prescribed, over-the-counter and recreational.
- ICE – patient ideas, concerns and expectations.
- Summary.
- Checks understanding.

- Asks if there are any questions.
- Uses appropriate closing.

Marks may also be awarded for :
- Rapport
- Appropriate body language
- Lack of jargon
- Empathy
- Active listening
- Considering the patient's perspective
- Fluidity of the consultation.

Giving Information

General
- Greeting – greets patient by name/checks they have the right patient.
- Introduction – introduces themselves and anyone else in the room, and explains their roles.

Starting Point
- Starting point – assesses what the patient knows already.
- How much? – assesses how much the patient wants to know.

Giving the Information
- Signpost – outlines areas to be covered.
- Chunk and check – gives small chunks of information at a time; checks understanding after each chunk.
- Summarises.
- Reinforces – reinforces the important points.
- Written information – provides leaflets, diagrams, etc.

Patient
- Relevant – makes the explanation relevant to the patient's circumstances.
- NICE – assesses the patient's Needs, Ideas, Concerns, Expectations.

Completing the Consultation
- Summarises.
- Checks understanding.
- Asks if there are any questions.
- Reinforces – restates the most important pieces of information.
- Appropriate closing statement.
- Safety net – provides a means for returning with future questions or problems.

Marks may also be awarded for:
- Rapport
- Appropriate body language
- Lack of jargon
- Empathy
- Active listening
- Considering the patient's perspective
- Fluidity of the consultation.

Informed Decision Making
General
- Greeting – greets patient by name/checks has correct patient
- Introduction – introduces themselves and anyone else in the room, and explains their roles.

Starting Point
- Starting point – assesses what patient already knows.
- How much? – assesses how much the patient wants to know.
- What role – assesses what role the patient wishes to take.

Giving the Information
- Signposts – outlines areas to be covered.
- Options
    - outlines options available
    - informs without bias
    - relates to patient's circumstances.
- Chunk and check – gives small chunks of information at a time; checks understanding after each chunk.

- Summarises.
- Reinforces – reinforces the important points.
- Gives written information – leaflets, diagrams, etc.

Patient
- Relevant – makes the information relevant to the patient's circumstances.
- NICE – Identifies patient's Needs, Ideas, Concerns, Expectations.

Completing the Consultation
- Summarises.
- Checks understanding.
- Checks if patient has any questions.
- Reinforces – restates the most important pieces of information.
- Uses appropriate closing statement.
- Safety net – provides a means for returning with future questions or problems.

Marks may also be awarded for:
- Rapport
- Appropriate body language
- Lack of jargon
- Empathy
- Active listening
- Considering the patient's perspective
- Fluidity of the consultation.

Breaking Bad News
General
- Greeting – greets patient by name/checks has correct patient.
- Introduction – introduces themselves and anyone else in the room, and explains their roles.

Starting Point
- Starting point – assesses what patient already knows/has been told.

Giving the Bad News
- Warning shot – gave warning of bad news.
- Breaks news factually.
- Allows bad news to settle – silence.
- Assesses patient's concerns/feelings/anxieties about the news.
- Checks patient's understanding of what has been discussed.
- Asks if patient has any questions.
- Assesses if patient ready to consider options/make decisions/plan.
- Ensures definite plan in place for next step.

Patient
- Relevant – makes the information given relevant to the patient's circumstances.
- NICE – Identifies patient's Needs, Ideas, Concerns, Expectations.

Completing the Consultation
- Summarises.
- Checks understanding.
- Checks if patient has any questions.
- Reinforces – restates the most important pieces of information.
- Uses appropriate closing statement .
- Safety net – provides a means for returning with future questions or problems.

Marks may also be awarded for:
- Rapport
- Appropriate body language
- Lack of jargon
- Empathy
- Active listening
- Considering the patient's perspective
  Fluidity of the consultation.

Further Reading

This book is designed as a revision aid only and will not provide the depth of information that is required for a really solid knowledge of clinical communication skills. Books can provide guidance on the skills to use in any situation, but no one would expect to be able to play a piano after only reading a book on the subject. As with the piano, the only way to improve your skills is to practise, practise, practise until you become better, and then practise some more.

For those of you who wish to lay down solid guidelines for your practice, the books listed below are recommended as both readable and relevant.

Bor, R., and Lloyd, M. (c.2004, reprinted 2005). *Communication Skills for Medicine*. Edinburgh: Churchill Livingstone

Dallas, J., Sully, P. and Nicol, M. (2005). *Essential Communication Skills for Nursing*. Edinburgh: Elsevier Mosby

Silverman, J., Kurtz, S. and Draper, J.(2005). *Skills for Communicating with Patients* (Second Edition). Abingdon: Radcliffe Medical Press

Tate, P. (2003). *The Doctor's Communication Handbook, Fourth Edition*. Abingdon: Radcliffe Medical Press

Tietze, K. J. (1997). *Clinical Skills for Pharmacists: A Patient-Focused Approach.* St. Louis, Mo.; London: Mosby